The Colors that Influence Marketing

I0401447

Practical guide

G. Dellis

Guide to effective marketing colors

1.Introduction

Color is a fundamental component of marketing and branding, with a significant impact on consumer perception and purchasing behavior. The psychology of color is a field of study that explores how different colors influence people's emotions and decisions. In the context of marketing, understanding the meaning of colors is essential for creating effective brand identities, engaging advertising campaigns, and eye-catching packaging.

The choice of colors is not random; it is a carefully studied strategy that can determine the success or failure of a product or brand. Colors evoke specific emotions, sensations, and associations that can vary depending on cultures, personal experiences, and social contexts. For example, red can evoke feelings of urgency and excitement, while blue is often associated with trust and professionalism.

This guide will explore the meaning of colors in marketing, analyzing how each color affects consumer behavior, the emotions evoked, and best practices for effectively using colors in marketing strategies. We will also see practical examples of how leading brands use colors to communicate their values and attract their target audience.

The Meaning of Colors in Marketing

Red

Red is a powerful color, often associated with intense emotions such as passion, energy, and urgency. In marketing, red is used to immediately capture attention and stimulate a sense of excitement or alarm. It is common to see red in sale promotions, advertising campaigns that require a quick response, and brands that want to convey a bold and dynamic personality.

For example, Coca-Cola uses red in its logo and packaging to evoke feelings of energy and conviviality. Red is also common in fast food restaurants, where it can stimulate appetite and accelerate the pace of customer consumption.

Blue

Blue is often associated with tranquility, trust, and professionalism. It is a calming color that can reduce anxiety and increase feelings of security. In marketing, blue is used by brands that want to be perceived as reliable and serious. It is common in sectors such as technology, finance, and healthcare, where customer trust is crucial.

Brands like IBM and Facebook use blue to convey a sense of stability and security. Blue can also foster a perception of high quality and competence, which is why it is often chosen by companies offering professional or technological services.

Green

Green symbolizes nature, growth, and health. It is a color that evokes tranquility and renewal, often associated with eco-friendly and sustainable products. In marketing, green is used to communicate concepts of wellness, freshness, and sustainability.

Brands like Starbucks and Whole Foods use green to emphasize their focus on natural quality and environmental responsibility. Additionally, green can convey a sense of relaxation and calm, making it a popular choice for products related to health and wellness.

Yellow

Yellow is a bright and stimulating color, often associated with happiness, optimism, and creativity. It is a color that can quickly attract attention and stimulate positive emotions. In marketing, yellow is used to convey energy, joy, and warmth.

Brands like IKEA and McDonald's use yellow to create a welcoming and lively atmosphere. Yellow is particularly effective in advertisements aimed at instilling a sense of positivity and cheerfulness in consumers.

Orange

Orange combines the energy of red with the happiness of yellow. It is a color associated with enthusiasm, creativity, and adventure. In marketing, orange is often used to attract attention without being too overwhelming. It is a friendly and inviting color that can stimulate conversations and interactions.

Brands like Nickelodeon and Fanta use orange to convey a sense of fun and lightheartedness. Orange is also effective in call-to-action buttons, such as purchase buttons, due to its ability to stimulate a sense of urgency without the pressure of red.

Purple

Purple is traditionally associated with royalty, luxury, and creativity. It is a color that evokes a sense of superior quality and uniqueness. In marketing, purple is used by brands that want to stand out for their sophistication and originality.

Brands like Cadbury and Hallmark use purple to communicate a sense of elegance and distinction. Purple is also effective in the beauty and wellness sectors, where it can convey a sense of luxury and attention to detail.

Black

Black is a powerful and sophisticated color, often associated with elegance, authority, and mystery. In marketing, black is used to convey a sense of luxury and refinement. It is a versatile color that can be used to create a modern and minimalist look or a more classic and traditional one.

High fashion brands like Chanel and Gucci use black to convey exclusivity and style. Black can also be used for technological products, where it can give a clean and professional appearance.

White

White represents purity, simplicity, and transparency. It is a color that evokes cleanliness and minimalism. In marketing, white is used to convey clarity and freshness, often in combination with other colors to create contrast and highlight design.

Brands like Apple and Nike use white to create a clean and modern aesthetic. White is particularly effective in products related to health and wellness, where it can suggest a sense of purity and simplicity.

Pink

Pink is a color associated with femininity, sweetness, and romance. In marketing, pink is used for products and brands that want to communicate delicacy, love, and care. It is common in the fashion, beauty, and children's product sectors.

Brands like Victoria's Secret and Barbie use pink to reinforce their feminine and attractive image. Pink can range from pastel to fuchsia, allowing for a wide range of emotional and stylistic expressions.

Brown

Brown is a color that evokes stability, reliability, and naturalness. In marketing, brown is used for products that want to communicate a connection with the earth and nature. It is common in sectors such as food and furniture, where it can suggest a sense of authenticity and sturdiness.

Brands like UPS and Hershey's use brown to convey trust and quality. Brown can also evoke a sense of comfort and security, making it an ideal choice for products related to home and family.

Practical Examples of the Use of Colors in Marketing

Coca-Cola: Red

Coca-Cola is one of the most iconic examples of the use of color in marketing. The red of the logo and packaging is immediately recognizable and conveys energy, passion, and conviviality. The choice of red has helped Coca-Cola position itself as a beverage that brings happiness and joyful moments. Coca-Cola's advertising campaigns often emphasize these feelings, creating a strong emotional association with the color red.

IBM: Blue

IBM, with its "Big Blue," uses blue to convey reliability, professionalism, and technological innovation. The blue in IBM's logo evokes a sense of trust and stability, fundamental qualities in a global technology company. The blue color helps reassure customers about the competence and reliability of IBM's services and products.

Starbucks: Green

Starbucks uses green to communicate a connection with nature and a commitment to sustainability. The green in Starbucks' logo evokes feelings of tranquility and well-being, positioning the brand as a healthy and responsible choice. This color supports Starbucks' mission to promote sustainable business practices and offer high-quality products.

McDonald's: Red and Yellow

McDonald's combines red and yellow to create a visual effect that stimulates appetite and invites action. Red captures attention and conveys energy, while yellow evokes happiness and warmth. This color combination is particularly effective in the restaurant industry, where the goal is to attract customers and encourage them to consume quickly.

Apple: White

Apple uses white to convey a clean, modern, and minimalist aesthetic. The white in Apple's packaging and stores creates a brand experience that emphasizes simplicity and innovation. This color helps Apple stand out as a premium brand that offers high-quality products with elegant design.

UPS: Brown

UPS chose brown for its branding to convey reliability and professionalism. The brown in UPS's vehicles and uniforms evokes a sense of security and stability, reinforcing the image of a solid and trustworthy logistics company. This color helps UPS differentiate itself in a competitive market by communicating high-quality service.

The meaning of colors in marketing is a crucial element for building a successful brand. Each color evokes specific emotions and perceptions, influencing how consumers interact with a product or brand. Understanding the psychology of color and applying it strategically can significantly improve the effectiveness of advertising campaigns, packaging design, and brand identity.

Brands that manage to use colors effectively can create lasting emotional connections with their audience, stand out from the competition, and drive purchasing behavior. In an increasingly crowded market, choosing the right color can be the key to capturing attention and building a trust relationship with consumers.

The in-depth analysis of the meanings of colors and practical examples of their use by leading brands demonstrates how important it is to integrate the psychology of color into marketing strategies. Whether it's evoking energy with red, conveying trust with blue, or promoting sustainability with green, each color has the power to tell a unique story and influence consumer decisions.

2.Cultural Associations with Colors and Color Psychology

Color is a fundamental element of our perception of the world, profoundly influencing our emotions, behavior, and decisions. In the context of marketing, advertising, and design, understanding cultural associations and the psychology of colors is essential for effectively communicating with diverse audiences. Each color carries a load of meanings that can vary significantly depending on cultural, historical, and personal contexts.

Cultural Associations with Colors

Colors do not have intrinsic meanings; they acquire meanings through cultural use and traditions. Cultural associations with colors can vary widely from one culture to another, making it crucial for marketers and designers to understand these differences to avoid misunderstandings and communicate effectively.

Red

- **West**: In many Western countries, red is associated with passion, energy, love, but also danger and aggression. It is commonly used to attract attention and create a sense of urgency.

- **Asia**: In China and many other Asian cultures, red is a color of luck, prosperity, and happiness. It is often used in celebrations such as the Chinese New Year and weddings.

- **India**: In India, red symbolizes purity and sensuality and is traditionally worn by brides at weddings.

Blue

- **West**: Blue is often associated with tranquility, trust, and professionalism. It is a widely used color by technology and finance companies to convey reliability and competence.

- **Middle East**: In many Middle Eastern cultures, blue is a protective color, often used in talismans against the evil eye.

- **Asia**: In some Asian cultures, blue can be associated with spirituality and immortality.

Green

- **West**: Green is commonly associated with nature, growth, health, and sustainability. It is widely used for eco-friendly products and environmental initiatives.

- **Islam**: In the Islamic world, green is a sacred color, associated with Muhammad and paradise.

- **Ireland**: In Ireland, green is a national color, associated with the shamrock and St. Patrick's Day.

Yellow

- **West**: Yellow is often associated with happiness, optimism, and creativity. However, it can also have negative connotations such as cowardice and warning.

- **Asia**: In many Asian cultures, yellow is an imperial and sacred color. In China, it was historically reserved for emperors.

- **Africa**: In some African countries, yellow is associated with wealth and luxury.

Black

- **West**: Black is generally associated with elegance, power, mystery, and mourning. It is widely used in fashion for its slimming and sophisticated effect.

- **Asia**: In some Asian cultures, black can be associated with bad luck and evil.

- **Africa**: In many African cultures, black can symbolize maturity and life.

White

- **West**: White is generally associated with purity, innocence, and peace. It is the traditional color of wedding dresses.

- **Asia**: In many Asian cultures, white is the color of mourning and death.

- **Africa**: In some African cultures, white can represent purity and spirituality.

Color Psychology

Color psychology studies how different colors influence human emotions and behaviors. This discipline is widely used in marketing, design, and advertising to evoke specific emotional responses and influence consumer decisions.

Red

Red is a stimulating color that can increase heart rate and create a sense of urgency. It is often used to capture attention and stimulate action.

- **Emotions evoked**: Passion, energy, excitement, aggression.

- **Use in marketing**: Call-to-action, sales, food products.

Blue

Blue is a calming color that can reduce anxiety and promote trust. It is widely used to convey serenity and professionalism.

- **Emotions evoked**: Tranquility, trust, security.

- **Use in marketing**: Technology companies, financial services, healthcare.

Green

Green is associated with nature and growth, evoking feelings of balance and renewal. It is often used for health and eco-friendly products.

- **Emotions evoked**: Renewal, balance, health.

- **Use in marketing**: Organic products, sustainable initiatives, wellness.

Yellow

Yellow is a bright color that stimulates happiness and optimism. However, it can also cause visual fatigue if overused.

- **Emotions evoked**: Joy, optimism, creativity.

- **Use in marketing**: Cheerful advertisements, children's products, youthful branding.

Orange

Orange combines the energy of red with the happiness of yellow, creating a color that stimulates enthusiasm and action.

- **Emotions evoked**: Enthusiasm, creativity, adventure.
- **Use in marketing**: Promotions, call-to-action, youth products.

Purple

Purple is a color that evokes luxury, creativity, and spirituality. It is often used for premium products and brands that want to convey a sense of exclusivity.

- **Emotions evoked**: Luxury, creativity, mystery.

- **Use in marketing**: Luxury products, cosmetics, creative brands.

Black

Black is associated with power, elegance, and mystery. It is widely used in high fashion design and technological products to create a sophisticated look.

- **Emotions evoked**: Power, elegance, mystery.

- **Use in marketing**: Fashion, luxury products, technology.

White

White evokes purity, simplicity, and clarity. It is often used to create a clean and modern design.

- **Emotions evoked**: Purity, simplicity, transparency.

- **Use in marketing**: Technology, healthcare, minimalist design.

Pink

Pink is a color associated with sweetness, femininity, and love. It is widely used in products and brands aimed at a female audience.

- **Emotions evoked**: Sweetness, love, tenderness.

- **Use in marketing**: Women's fashion, beauty products, children's branding.

Brown

Brown evokes stability, reliability, and naturalness. It is often used for products that want to communicate a connection to the earth and tradition.

- **Emotions evoked**: Stability, reliability, comfort.

- **Use in marketing**: Food products, home goods, traditional branding.

3.Psychological Effects of Colors on User Behavior

Using Colors to Influence Consumer Emotions

Color is a powerful psychological tool that profoundly affects people's emotions, perceptions, and behaviors. In the fields of marketing and commerce, colors are strategically used to evoke specific emotional responses in consumers, influencing their purchasing decisions and how they perceive brands. Understanding color psychology allows companies to create effective advertising campaigns, attractive packaging, and optimized retail environments to maximize sales.

Psychological Effects of Colors on User Behavior

Colors can evoke specific emotions and

moods, and these psychological reactions can significantly influence user behavior. The following analysis explores how different colors can affect consumer behavior.

Red

Red is one of the most powerful and visible colors, capable of eliciting a wide range of emotions and behavioral reactions.

- **Excitement and Urgency**: Red is often associated with intense emotions such as passion, excitement, and urgency. This makes it ideal for promotions and sales, where the goal is to quickly capture the consumer's attention and stimulate action.

- **Appetite**: Red is also known to stimulate appetite, which is why it is commonly used in restaurants and fast-food chains. Examples include McDonald's and KFC.

- **Increased Heart Rate**: Red can increase

heart rate, creating a sense of energy and urgency that can push consumers to make quick decisions.

Blue

Blue is a color that tends to evoke feelings of calm and security, making it ideal for industries that require consumer trust.

- **Reliability and Trust**: Blue is often used by technology, financial, and healthcare companies to convey reliability and security. Examples include IBM, Visa, and many banks.

- **Calm and Serenity**: Blue has a calming effect, reducing anxiety and promoting a sense of tranquility. This can be particularly useful in retail environments to create a relaxing shopping experience.

- **Professionalism**: Blue is also associated with professionalism and competence, which is why it is widely used in corporate and technology sectors.

Green

Green is often associated with nature, growth, and health, making it an ideal color for products and brands that want to convey these values.

- **Well-being and Health**: Green is commonly used for eco-friendly, organic, and health-related products. Examples include Whole Foods and natural beauty products.

- **Tranquility and Renewal**: Green has a calming effect and can evoke feelings of tranquility and renewal. This makes it ideal for environments that promote relaxation and well-being, such as spas and wellness centers.

- **Sustainability**: Green is associated with sustainability and environmental responsibility, making it a common choice for companies that want to promote eco-friendly practices.

Yellow

Yellow is a bright and stimulating color that can evoke feelings of happiness and optimism.

- **Happiness and Optimism**: Yellow is often used in advertising that aims to convey joy and positivity. Examples include summer campaigns and children's products.

- **Attention**: Yellow is highly visible and can quickly attract attention. This makes it useful for signage and promotional displays.

- **Mental Stimulation**: Yellow can stimulate mental activity and increase the feeling of energy, making it useful for environments that encourage creativity and interaction.

Orange

Orange combines the energy of red with the happiness of yellow, creating a color that stimulates enthusiasm and action.

- **Enthusiasm and Creativity**: Orange is often associated with creativity, enthusiasm, and adventure. It is used in advertising campaigns that aim to spark interest and excitement.

- **Action**: Orange can stimulate the desire for action, making it ideal for call-to-action and promotions. Examples include online purchase buttons and sale signage.

- **Accessibility**: Orange is perceived as a friendly and accessible color, making it a popular choice for brands that want to convey a welcoming and inclusive image.

Purple

Purple is a color that evokes luxury, creativity, and mystery, making it ideal for brands that want to convey a sense of exclusivity and sophistication.

- **Luxury and Elegance**: Purple is often used for luxury products and brands that want to communicate superior quality and exclusivity. Examples include high-end beauty and fashion products.

- **Creativity**: Purple is also associated with creativity and originality, making it a common choice for brands that want to stand out for their innovation and uniqueness.

- **Spirituality**: Purple can evoke feelings of spirituality and introspection, making it suitable for products related to meditation and spiritual well-being.

Black

Black is a powerful and sophisticated color that can convey elegance, authority, and mystery.

- **Elegance and Luxury**: Black is often used in high fashion design and luxury products to create a sophisticated and exclusive look. Examples include fashion brands like Chanel and Gucci.

- **Authority and Power**: Black can also convey a sense of authority and power, making it ideal for industries that require a strong presence, such as technology and automotive.

- **Minimalism**: Black is used in minimalist designs to create a clean and modern look, as seen in Apple's technological products.

White

White is a color that represents purity, simplicity, and transparency. It is often used to create a clean and modern design.

- **Purity and Innocence**: White is often used for health and beauty products where purity is a core value. Examples include hygiene products and cosmetics.

- **Simplicity and Clarity**: White can create a clean and simple look, making it ideal for modern and minimalist designs. It is widely used in Apple's packaging and retail stores.

- **Transparency and Neutrality**: White can convey transparency and neutrality, making it a common choice for brands that want to communicate honesty and openness.

Pink

Pink is a color associated with sweetness, femininity, and love. It is widely used in products and brands aimed at a female audience.

- **Sweetness and Tenderness**: Pink is often used in products for children and cosmetics to convey sweetness and tenderness. Examples include Barbie and Victoria's Secret.

- **Femininity**: Pink is commonly associated with femininity, making it a popular choice for brands targeting a female audience.

- **Romanticism**: Pink can evoke feelings of love and romance, making it ideal for products related to Valentine's Day and romantic occasions.

Brown

Brown is a color that evokes stability, reliability, and naturalness. It is often used for products that want to communicate a connection with the earth and tradition.

- **Stability and Reliability**: Brown is often used for products that want to communicate stability and reliability, such as UPS and Hershey's.

- **Naturalness**: Brown is associated with the earth and nature, making it ideal for eco-friendly and organic products. Examples include organic foods and rustic furniture.

- **Comfort**: Brown can evoke a sense of comfort and security, making it a popular choice for home and family-related products.

Using Colors to Influence Consumer Emotions in Commerce and Marketing

Understanding the psychological effects of colors allows marketers to create targeted strategies that positively influence consumer emotions and, consequently, their purchasing decisions. Let's see how colors are used in commerce and marketing to achieve these goals.

Advertising and Promotions

Colors are used in advertising campaigns to capture attention and stimulate consumers' emotions, guiding them towards the desired action.

- **Sales and Offers**: Red is often used in promotions to create a sense of urgency and stimulate immediate action. Examples include sale billboards and online advertising banners.

- **Summer Products**: Yellow and orange are commonly used in summer advertising campaigns to evoke feelings of happiness and adventure. Examples include advertisements for beverages and travel.

- **Luxury and Elegance**: Black and purple are used in advertising campaigns for luxury products to convey sophistication and exclusivity. Examples include high-end perfumes and jewelry.

Packaging

The color of packaging can significantly influence purchasing decisions by creating an immediate emotional connection with the product.

- **Food and Beverages**: Red and yellow are commonly used in food and beverage packaging to stimulate appetite and capture attention. Examples include snack and drink packaging.

- **Beauty Products**: Pink and purple are used in beauty product packaging to evoke feelings of femininity and luxury. Examples include cosmetics and perfumes.

- **Natural Products**: Green and brown are used in eco-friendly and organic product packaging to communicate naturalness and sustainability. Examples include organic foods and skincare products.

Store Design

Color can be used in store design to create an environment that positively influences consumer behavior.

- **Restaurants**: Restaurants often use warm colors like red and orange to stimulate appetite and create a welcoming atmosphere. Examples include fast-food chains.

- **Fashion Stores**: High-end fashion stores often use neutral and sophisticated colors like black and white to create an elegant and refined environment. Examples include luxury boutiques.

- **Supermarkets**: Supermarkets use a variety of colors to guide consumers through the store and draw attention to offers and promotions. Examples include colorful sections for fresh produce and sales.

Colors are powerful tools in marketing and commerce, capable of deeply influencing consumer emotions and behaviors. Understanding color psychology and cultural color associations allows marketers to create effective strategies that enhance the consumer experience and increase sales.

By strategically using colors, brands can create lasting emotional connections with their customers, convey brand values, and guide purchasing decisions. Whether evoking energy with red, conveying trust with blue, or promoting sustainability with green, each color has the power to tell a unique story and significantly influence consumer emotions.

In an increasingly competitive market, the ability to effectively use colors can be the key to standing out from the competition and building a successful brand.

4.Practical Applications of Colors in Marketing

Color is one of the most powerful tools available to marketers. Colors can evoke emotions, influence perceptions and behaviors, and create lasting connections between consumers and brands. Understanding the practical applications of colors in marketing is essential for creating effective strategies that not only attract attention but also communicate the desired message and stimulate consumer action. In this article, we will explore in detail how colors are used in branding, advertising, packaging design, store design, and digital marketing.

Branding and Visual Identity

Creating Brand Identity

Color is a crucial component of a brand's

visual identity. Choosing the right color can make a brand instantly recognizable and help communicate the brand's values and personality. For example:

- **Coca-Cola**: Red is the dominant color of the Coca-Cola brand, evoking energy, passion, and excitement. This color helps make the brand recognizable worldwide.

- **Facebook**: Blue is used by Facebook to convey trust and security, key elements for a platform that handles sensitive personal information.

- **Starbucks**: The green in the Starbucks logo represents sustainability and health, positioning the brand as an eco-friendly and healthy choice for coffee.

Differentiation and Positioning

Color can also be used to differentiate a brand from its competitors and position it uniquely in the market. For example:

- **T-Mobile**: Uses magenta, a distinctive color in the telecommunications sector, to differentiate itself from competitors like AT&T (blue) and Verizon (red).

- **Cadbury**: Chose purple to convey luxury and premium quality, distinguishing itself from other chocolate brands.

Advertising and Promotions

Capturing Attention

Bright and contrasting colors are often used in advertising campaigns to capture consumers' attention. For example:

- **Sales Promotions**: Red is commonly used to signal sales and special offers, creating a sense of urgency and encouraging immediate action.

- **Seasonal Advertising Campaigns**: Yellow and orange are frequently used in summer campaigns to evoke feelings of warmth, happiness, and adventure.

Communicating Specific Messages

Colors can help communicate specific messages and evoke desired emotions. For example:

- **Health and Wellness Campaigns**: Green is often used to promote health and wellness products and services, evoking feelings of naturalness and tranquility.

- **Luxury Products**: Black and purple are used to communicate sophistication and exclusivity in luxury products.

Packaging Design

Visual Appeal

Packaging design is crucial for attracting consumers' attention on store shelves. Colors play a critical role in this process. For example:

- **Food and Beverages**: Red and yellow are commonly used in snack and beverage packaging to stimulate appetite and capture attention. Examples include chip bags and soda cans.

- **Beauty Products**: Pink and purple are used in cosmetic packaging to convey femininity and luxury. Examples include perfumes and skincare products.

Conveying Information

Colors can also be used to convey important information about products. For example:

- **Organic Products**: Green is commonly used to indicate that a product is eco-friendly or organic. Examples include organic food labels and natural skincare packaging.

- **Health Products**: Blue and white are often used to convey purity and safety in healthcare and pharmaceutical products. Examples include medication packaging and hygiene products.

Store Design

Creating Specific Atmospheres

Color can influence the atmosphere of a store and, consequently, consumer behavior. For example:

- **Restaurants**: Restaurants often use warm colors like red and orange to stimulate appetite and create a welcoming environment. Examples include fast food chains like McDonald's and Burger King.

- **Fashion Stores**: High-end fashion stores often use neutral and sophisticated colors like black and white to create an elegant and refined atmosphere. Examples include luxury boutiques.

Guiding and Orienting Customers

Colors can be used to guide customers through a store and draw attention to specific products or promotions. For example:

- **Supermarkets**: Supermarkets use a variety of colors to differentiate sections and guide customers. Examples include green for fresh produce sections and red for promotional areas.

- **Department Stores**: Department stores use bright and contrasting colors to signal sales and promotions, attracting customers' attention.

Digital Marketing

Websites and Apps

Website and app design is an area where color plays a crucial role in enhancing user experience and guiding interaction. For example:

- **Call-to-Action Buttons**: Call-to-action (CTA) buttons often use bright colors like red, orange, or green to attract attention and encourage users to take a specific action, such as making a purchase or signing up for a newsletter.

- **App Design**: Apps use colors to enhance navigation and usability. For example, fitness apps may use energizing colors like orange to motivate users, while meditation apps may use blue and green shades to create a relaxing environment.

Social Media

Colors are strategically used on social media to create visually appealing content that captures users' attention. For example:

- **Images and Graphics**: Images and graphics with bright and contrasting colors tend to have higher engagement on platforms like Instagram and Facebook.

- **Social Media Branding**: Brands use colors consistent with their visual identity to reinforce brand recognition and create a cohesive and attractive feed. For example, a fashion brand's Instagram feed might use a specific color palette to maintain a uniform aesthetic.

Practical Applications in Specific Industries

Food Industry

Color plays a crucial role in the food industry, influencing not only the visual appeal of products but also perceptions of taste and quality.

- **Red and Yellow**: Used to stimulate appetite and create a sense of urgency. Fast food chains like McDonald's and Burger King use these colors to attract customers and stimulate appetite.

- **Green**: Used to convey health and freshness, often employed in organic and natural products. Examples include Whole Foods and other grocery chains promoting health.

Fashion Industry

Color is essential in the fashion industry to communicate style, season, and garment quality.

- **Black**: Used to convey elegance and sophistication, commonly seen in high fashion collections and luxury boutiques. Examples include brands like Chanel and Prada.

- **Pastel Colors**: Used in spring and summer collections to evoke lightness and freshness. Examples include collections from brands like Zara and H&M.

Technology Industry

In the technology sector, colors are used to convey reliability, innovation, and professionalism.

- **Blue**: Often used by tech companies to convey security and trust. Examples include IBM, Dell, and Intel.

- **Black and Silver**: Used to convey modernity and innovation in tech products. Examples include Apple and Sony.

Beauty Industry

Color is fundamental in the beauty industry to attract attention and communicate product quality.

- **Pink and Purple**: Used to convey femininity and luxury. Examples include cosmetic brands like L'Oréal and Estée Lauder.

- **Gold and Silver**: Used for high-end products to convey exclusivity and superior quality. Examples include luxury brands like Dior and Chanel.

Case Studies

McDonald's

McDonald's uses a combination of red and yellow in its branding, packaging, and restaurants. Red stimulates appetite and creates a sense of urgency, while yellow evokes happiness and optimism. This color combination has been crucial to the brand's global success, attracting customers and driving sales.

Apple

Apple uses white, black, and gray in its products and store design to convey modernity, elegance, and simplicity. The minimalist design and color choice have helped create a sophisticated and innovative brand image, differentiating Apple from its competitors and creating a strong visual identity.

Tiffany & Co.

Tiffany & Co. is known for its distinctive "Tiffany Blue," used in branding and packaging. This unique color conveys luxury, quality, and tradition, helping create an exclusive and recognizable brand image. Tiffany Blue has become synonymous with elegance and refinement, reinforcing the brand's position in the luxury jewelry market.

Color is an essential tool in marketing, with the ability to profoundly influence consumer perceptions and behaviors. From creating brand identity to designing effective advertising campaigns, color plays a crucial role in every aspect of marketing. Understanding the practical applications of colors allows marketers to create visually appealing strategies that communicate brand values, attract consumers, and drive action.

In an increasingly competitive market, the effective use of colors can be the key to standing out from the competition and building a successful brand. Whether it's evoking emotions with red, conveying trust with blue, or promoting sustainability with green, each color has the power to tell a unique story and create lasting emotional connections with consumers.

5.Use of Colors in Branding

Color is one of the most powerful and immediate elements in branding. Choosing the right colors can determine the success of a brand by influencing consumer perceptions, emotions, and purchase decisions. This article explores in detail the role of colors in branding, analyzing how and why colors are used, their psychological and cultural implications, and how brands can leverage this knowledge to create strong and coherent brand identities.

The Role of Colors in Branding

Perception and Memorability

One of the main reasons colors are so crucial in branding is their ability to influence perception and memorability. Colors can make a brand instantly recognizable and memorable. For example, a distinctive color can differentiate a brand from its competitors and stay in consumers' minds, facilitating brand recognition.

Conveying Messages and Values

Colors have the power to communicate a brand's messages and values without using words. Each color evokes specific sensations and emotions, which can be used to convey the brand's personality and values. For example, blue can communicate trust and security, green can evoke feelings of nature and sustainability, while red can convey energy and passion.

Influence on Emotions and Purchase Decisions

Colors influence emotions and, consequently, purchase decisions. Consumers tend to prefer and feel attracted to products and brands that use colors that evoke positive emotions.

Choosing the right colors can increase a product's attractiveness and encourage consumers to make a purchase.

Color Psychology in Branding

Blue

Blue is one of the most used colors in branding due to its positive associations. It is often associated with trust, security, professionalism, and tranquility. It is a color that inspires calm and stability, making it ideal for brands that want to convey reliability and security.

- **Practical Applications**: Blue is commonly used in industries such as technology, finance, and healthcare. It can be seen in logos, websites, and promotional materials of companies that want to be perceived as professional and reliable.

Red

Red is a powerful and dynamic color, often associated with energy, passion, excitement, and urgency. It is a color that immediately attracts attention and can stimulate strong emotions.

- **Practical Applications**: Red is used in the branding of food products, beverages, entertainment, and fashion. It is effective in promotions and sales as it creates a sense of urgency and stimulates action.

Green

Green is a color associated with nature, growth, health, and sustainability. It evokes feelings of calm, balance, and freshness.

- **Practical Applications**: Green is often used by brands that want to be associated with eco-friendly, natural, or healthy products. It is common in the organic food, health and wellness, and eco-friendly products sectors.

Yellow

Yellow is a bright and positive color, associated with happiness, optimism, and creativity. It is a color that attracts attention and can evoke feelings of joy and warmth.

- **Practical Applications**: Yellow is used in the branding of children's products, toys, summer products, and advertising campaigns that want to convey positivity and energy.

Black

Black is a sophisticated and elegant color, often associated with luxury, power, and modernity. It is a color that conveys authority and refinement.

- **Practical Applications**: Black is commonly used in the branding of luxury products, fashion, technology, and high-end automobiles. It is ideal for brands that want to be perceived as exclusive and prestigious.

White

White is a color associated with purity, simplicity, and transparency. It evokes feelings of cleanliness and minimalism.

- **Practical Applications**: White is used in the branding of beauty products, health, technology, and design. It is effective in conveying simplicity and modernity.

Cultural Associations of Colors in Branding

Colors do not have the same meaning in all cultures. It is important to consider the cultural associations of colors when developing a global branding strategy.

West

- **Blue**: Trust, professionalism, security.

- **Red**: Passion, excitement, urgency.

- **Green**: Nature, health, sustainability.

- **Yellow**: Happiness, optimism, creativity.

- **Black**: Elegance, power, luxury.

- **White**: Purity, simplicity, cleanliness.

Asia

- **Blue**: Immortality, harmony.

- **Red**: Good fortune, prosperity, happiness.

- **Green**: Nature, life, harmony.

- **Yellow**: Royalty, authority, respect.

- **Black**: Mystery, elegance, power.

- **White**: Death, mourning (in some Asian cultures, white is associated with mourning and death).

Middle East

- **Blue**: Protection, spirituality.

- **Red**: Danger, caution.

- **Green**: Islam, paradise, fertility.

- **Yellow**: Happiness, prosperity.

- **Black**: Mystery, grief.

- **White**: Purity, peace.

Color-Based Branding Strategies

Creating Color Palettes

Creating a coherent color palette is essential for effective branding. A well-chosen color palette can help maintain visual consistency across all marketing materials and create a recognizable brand identity.

- **Primary and Secondary**: A brand's color palette should include primary colors that represent the main identity of the brand, and secondary colors that complement and support the primary colors.

- **Contrasting and Complementary**: Using contrasting and complementary colors can create an attractive visual effect and improve readability and attention.

Adapting Colors to Marketing Channels

Colors can appear differently on various marketing channels, such as print, web, and packaging. It is important to consider how the chosen colors will appear in different contexts and ensure they are consistent and recognizable across all channels.

- **Print**: Printed colors can appear differently from those displayed on a screen. It is important to use precise color codes (such as CMYK for print) to ensure consistency.

- **Web**: Colors on the web can vary depending on devices and monitor settings. Use RGB or HEX color codes to ensure visual consistency.

- **Packaging**: Packaging colors must be consistent with the brand's visual identity and attract attention on store shelves. Use materials and finishes that enhance the chosen colors.

Implementing Colors in Branding

Logo

The logo is one of the most important

elements of a brand's visual identity. Choosing the colors in the logo can deeply influence the brand's perception.

- **Recognizability**: Use distinctive colors that make the logo easily recognizable.

- **Consistency**: Ensure that the logo colors are consistent with the brand's color palette and reflect the brand's values and personality.

Website

The website is often the first point of contact between the consumer and the brand. The colors of the website must be carefully chosen to create a pleasant and coherent user experience.

- **Navigation**: Use colors that facilitate navigation and improve readability.

- **CTA (Call to Action)**: Use contrasting

colors for call-to-action buttons to attract attention and encourage interaction.

Promotional Materials

Promotional materials, such as brochures, flyers, and advertisements, must use the brand colors consistently to reinforce the visual identity and attract consumer attention.

- **Visibility**: Use bright and contrasting colors to attract attention.

- **Consistency**: Ensure that the colors used in promotional materials are consistent with the brand's color palette.

Social Media

Social media is an important channel for branding and promotion. The colors used in social media content must be consistent with the brand's visual identity and attract user attention.

- **Feed Consistency**: Use a consistent color palette to create an attractive and recognizable feed.

- **Images and Graphics**: Use bright and captivating colors in images and graphics to increase engagement.

Packaging

Packaging is a crucial element of branding, as it represents the physical point of contact between the consumer and the product. Packaging colors must be chosen to attract attention, communicate brand values, and differentiate the product from competitors.

- **Visual Appeal**: Use colors that attract attention on shelves and entice consumers to pick up the product.

- **Information**: Use colors to differentiate different product variants and convey important information, such as ingredients or special features.

The use of colors in branding is a fundamental component of any company's marketing strategy. Colors have the power to influence consumers' perceptions, emotions, and purchase decisions. Understanding the psychology of colors and cultural associations is essential to creating a strong and coherent brand identity.

From creating a balanced color palette to consistently implementing colors across all marketing channels, brands can leverage the power of colors to stand out from the competition, attract and retain consumers, and effectively communicate their values and messages.

Attention to detail in choosing and using colors can make the difference between a brand that blends into the crowd and one that stands out and leaves a lasting impression. By using colors strategically and consciously, brands can build a strong and recognizable visual presence that resonates with their target audience and supports their business goals.

6. Choosing Colors for Marketing Materials (Websites, Logos, Packaging, etc.)

The choice of colors in marketing materials is crucial for influencing consumer perceptions, communicating brand values, and stimulating the desired action. This article explores in detail how colors are selected and effectively used in various marketing materials, including websites, logos, packaging, and more. We will analyze the psychology of colors, strategies for choosing colors, and provide practical examples to illustrate the impact of colors in marketing materials.

The Psychology of Colors in Marketing Materials

Importance of Color Psychology

Color psychology studies how colors influence emotions, perceptions, and human behavior. Colors are not just visual elements but powerful conveyors of meaning that can communicate deep messages and influence purchasing decisions.

- **Emotional Associations**: Each color evokes specific emotions and sensations. For example, blue can convey calmness and trust, while red can induce excitement and urgency.

- **Culturally Specific**: Associations with colors can vary significantly across cultures and regions. It is important to consider the cultural implications of colors when developing marketing materials for a global audience.

Applications of Colors in Marketing Materials

Marketing materials use colors in different ways to achieve specific objectives, such as attracting attention, communicating a message, and stimulating an action. Each type of material requires a unique color strategy to maximize visual and communicative impact.

Websites

Choosing Colors for Websites

Choosing colors for a website is essential to create a pleasant and consistent user experience. The colors must reflect the brand's identity and facilitate user navigation.

- **Key Considerations**:

  - **Brand Chromatism**: Use the brand's primary colors to maintain visual consistency.

  - **Contrast and Readability**: Ensure that texts are readable on colored backgrounds and that there is a good contrast between text and background.

  - **Evoked Emotions**: Choose colors that evoke the desired emotions in users. For example, green for an eco-friendly product site can convey sustainability and freshness.

Practical Example

For a website promoting natural and sustainable products, such as organic cosmetics, a predominant green color might be chosen. Green evokes nature, health, and sustainability, creating a visual experience that reflects the brand's values and attracts consumers interested in eco-friendly products.

Logos

Importance of Colors in Logos

The logo is the most recognizable visual element of a brand. The choice of colors in the logo must be carefully considered to reflect the brand's identity and values.

- **Recognizability**: Use distinctive colors that make the logo easily recognizable.

- **Consistency with Branding**: Ensure that the logo's colors are consistent with the brand's color palette to create a cohesive visual identity.

- **Color Psychology**: Choose colors that convey the desired emotions and messages. For example, blue for reliability and professionalism, or red for dynamism and energy.

Practical Example

For a logo of an innovative and reliable technology brand, the color blue might be chosen. Blue communicates trust, security, and professionalism, reflecting the brand's serious and reliable approach in the technology sector.

Packaging

Choosing Colors for Packaging

Packaging is the physical point of contact between the product and the consumer. Packaging colors must attract attention on the shelves and communicate product characteristics.

- **Visual Attractiveness**: Use bright and appealing colors to distinguish the product from the competition.

- **Communication of Features**: Packaging colors can convey information about the product, such as freshness, luxury, or practicality.

- **Brand Consistency**: Ensure that packaging colors are consistent with the overall brand visual identity.

Practical Example

For an organic and fresh food product,

packaging with shades of green and brown might be chosen. Green communicates naturalness and sustainability, while brown can evoke a sense of genuineness and tradition, suitable for a product that promotes organic and high-quality ingredients.

Promotional Materials

Using Colors in Promotional Materials

Promotional materials, such as brochures, flyers, and posters, use colors to capture attention and convey crucial information to consumers.

- **Attractive Design**: Use vibrant and contrasting colors to draw attention to promotional materials.

- **Clarity and Readability**: Ensure that the chosen colors do not compromise text readability.

- **Brand Consistency**: Maintain visual consistency by using the brand's color palette.

Practical Example

For a promotional campaign of a summer event, such as a music festival, vibrant colors like orange and yellow might be used. These colors evoke the energy and warmth of summer, attracting attention and creating a positive association with the event.

Strategies for Choosing Colors

Key Considerations

- **Target Market**: Understand the target audience and their cultural and emotional preferences regarding colors.

- **Brand Objectives**: Define which emotions and messages you want to communicate through the chosen colors.

- **Visual Consistency**: Maintain visual consistency across all marketing materials to reinforce the brand identity.

- **Testing and Feedback**: Test different color combinations and gather feedback to assess visual and communicative effectiveness.

Conclusions

Choosing colors in marketing materials is an essential component for the success of a branding strategy. Colors not only enhance the visual appeal of materials but can also profoundly influence consumer perceptions and purchasing decisions. Understanding the psychology of colors and implementing effective color strategies can help brands stand out from the competition, create a recognizable visual identity, and build lasting relationships with consumers.

Color choice is not just an aesthetic matter but a powerful form of visual communication that can make the difference between an effective marketing campaign and one that goes unnoticed.

7.Consequences of Color Choice in Advertising Campaigns

The choice of colors in advertising campaigns is a crucial component of marketing, profoundly influencing consumer perceptions, emotions, and actions. This article explores the consequences of color choices in advertising campaigns in detail, analyzing how colors can be strategically used to enhance campaign effectiveness and achieve marketing objectives. We will examine the psychology of colors, strategies for selecting colors, and provide practical examples to illustrate the impact of colors in advertising campaigns.

Psychology of Colors in Advertising Campaigns

Meaning and Emotions of Colors

Colors have the power to evoke deep emotions and sensations in consumers, influencing their perceptions and purchasing decisions. Color psychology studies how different colors are perceived and how they can affect human behavior.

Red: Symbolizes passion, energy, urgency. It is often used to grab attention and stimulate immediate action.

Blue: Represents trust, security, seriousness. It is a color that communicates professionalism and reliability.

Green: Evokes nature, health, sustainability. It is associated with eco-friendly products and healthy lifestyles.

Yellow: Symbolizes joy, optimism, creativity. It is a color that can attract attention and create a positive atmosphere.

Black: Represents elegance, luxury, exclusivity. It is often used for high-end products.

White: Symbolizes purity, simplicity, cleanliness. It is a color that conveys clarity and order.

Cultural Implications

Color associations can vary significantly

across cultures. It is essential to consider the cultural implications of colors in global advertising campaigns to avoid misunderstandings or misinterpretations.

East: For example, red is often associated with good luck and prosperity in many East Asian cultures.

West: Whereas in the West, it may be seen as a color that evokes passion or urgency.

Strategic Use of Colors

To maximize the effectiveness of advertising campaigns, it is essential to choose colors based on specific marketing objectives and the target audience.

Strategies for Choosing Colors in Advertising Campaigns

Emotional Engagement

Colors can be used to create an emotional connection with the target audience, eliciting emotions that stimulate interest and action.

Example: An advertising campaign for an energy product might use red to evoke energy and motivation, encouraging consumers to try the product to feel energized.

Differentiation from Competition

Colors can help distinguish a brand or product from competitors, creating a unique and recognizable visual identity.

Example: In a market saturated with tech products, a brand might use blue to convey trust and distinguish itself from competitors who use more vibrant or non-traditional colors.

Reflecting Brand Values

Colors must reflect the brand's values and personality, reinforcing the brand identity and creating visual consistency across all advertising campaigns.

Example: A natural cosmetics brand might use green to communicate sustainability and the use of natural ingredients, attracting consumers interested in an eco-friendly lifestyle.

Practical Implementation of Colors in Advertising Campaigns

Print and Publications

In printed publications, such as magazines and newspapers, colors should be chosen to capture user attention and effectively communicate the campaign message.

Example: An airline campaign might use blue and white to communicate the safety, comfort, and reliability of travel.

Digital Marketing

In digital marketing, such as online ads and social media, colors must be visually appealing to capture user attention and encourage interaction.

Example: A fitness app campaign might use yellow and green to evoke vitality and health, incentivizing users to download the app and start a fitness journey.

Video and Multimedia

In video ads and multimedia materials, colors should be used to create a memorable visual impact and stimulate action from viewers.

Example: A promotional video for a new line of beauty products might use pink and white to convey femininity, freshness, and luxury.

Case Study: Advertising Campaign for an Organic Food Product

Imagine an advertising campaign for a new organic breakfast cereal.

Chosen Colors: Green and brown.

Reasoning: Green evokes nature, health, and sustainability, ideal for an organic product. Brown communicates genuineness, naturalness, and authenticity of ingredients.

Objective: Attract consumers interested in a healthy and sustainable lifestyle, communicating the use of organic and natural ingredients.

The choice of colors in advertising campaigns significantly impacts the success of marketing strategies. Using colors strategically can enhance campaign effectiveness, create a distinctive visual identity, and emotionally connect with the target audience. It is essential to understand color psychology, consider cultural implications, and adapt color choices to the brand's specific objectives and audience characteristics.

Marketers who master the art of color choice can positively influence consumer perceptions, increase engagement, and drive sales. Investing time and resources in accurately selecting colors in advertising campaigns can make the difference between a memorable and successful campaign and one that gets lost in the market noise.

8.How to Choose the Right Colors and Avoid Mistakes

Choosing the right colors is essential for the success of marketing strategies. Colors are not just aesthetic elements but powerful tools that influence consumer perceptions, emotions, and actions. This article explores in detail how to choose the right colors for marketing, avoiding common mistakes and maximizing the visual and communicative impact of campaigns.

Importance of Color Choice in Marketing

Colors are fundamental in marketing for several reasons:

Visual Communication: Colors immediately communicate the tone and personality of the brand.

Differentiation: They help distinguish a brand from competitors.

Emotional Engagement: They can evoke

specific emotions in consumers.

Brand Recognition: They contribute to creating a recognizable visual identity.

Psychology of Colors in Marketing

Emotional and Cultural Associations

Each color evokes specific emotions and sensations:

Red: Passion, energy, urgency.

Blue: Trust, seriousness, calm.

Green: Health, nature, sustainability.

Yellow: Optimism, joy, energy.

Black: Elegance, luxury, mystery.

White: Purity, simplicity, cleanliness.

Color associations can vary significantly between cultures and regions of the world. It is important to consider the cultural implications of colors in global marketing strategies.

How to Choose the Right Colors

1. Understand the Target Audience

The first consideration in choosing colors is the target audience. It is essential to understand the preferences, emotions, and perceptions of the audience you are targeting.

Example: A brand targeting a young and dynamic audience might use vibrant and energetic colors like yellow or orange to capture attention and communicate a sense of youth and vitality.

2. Reflect Brand Values

The chosen colors must reflect the brand's values, mission, and personality.

Example: An eco-friendly brand might use green to communicate sustainability and respect for the environment, establishing a direct connection with its ideals.

3. Visual Consistency

Maintaining visual consistency across all

marketing materials is crucial for reinforcing brand identity.

Example: Using a consistent color palette across all communication channels, including websites, social media, packaging, and print advertising, to create a cohesive and memorable brand experience.

4. Consider Context and Usage

Colors should be chosen based on the context of use and the function of the marketing material.

Example: In a luxury product campaign, such as jewelry or watches, using elegant colors like black and gold can enhance the perception of exclusivity and quality.

5. Test and Optimize

It is important to test different color combinations and gather feedback to evaluate the visual and communicative effectiveness of the choices made.

Example: Conducting A/B tests on online ads to compare the impact of two different color palettes on users and optimizing future campaigns based on the results obtained.

Common Mistakes to Avoid in Color Choice

1. Ignoring Cultural Implications

Failing to consider cultural differences in color interpretation can lead to misunderstandings or negative perceptions of the brand.

Example: Using white for purity in the West, but for mourning in some Asian cultures.

2. Lack of Visual Consistency

Using different colors inconsistently across various marketing materials can confuse consumers and weaken brand identity.

Example: A website with a vibrant and bold color palette contrasting with minimalist and neutral packaging can create visual dissonance that disrupts the consumer experience.

3. Choosing Colors Based on Personal Preferences

Choosing colors based solely on personal preferences instead of branding considerations and the target audience can compromise the effectiveness of the marketing strategy.

Example: A marketing director who prefers red might insist on this color for a campaign, even if it does not align with the desired values and emotions for the target audience.

4. Not Testing Color Choices

Failing to test and evaluate the effectiveness of color choices can mean missing opportunities for improvement and optimization of advertising campaigns.

Example: Not gathering feedback from consumers or monitoring campaign performance metrics to understand the impact of the chosen colors.

Practical Examples of Good Color Choices

Fitness Center Campaign

Objective: Attract young adults interested in dynamic and modern fitness.

Color Choice: Yellow and black.

Reasoning: Yellow evokes energy and optimism, while black adds a touch of elegance and modernity.

Implementation: Use yellow to highlight the benefits of fitness and black to emphasize the exclusivity of the services offered.

Organic Product Campaign

Objective: Communicate naturalness and sustainability.

Color Choice: Green and brown.

Reasoning: Green symbolizes nature and sustainability, while brown adds a sense of authenticity and genuineness of ingredients.

Implementation: Use green to convey the benefits of the organic product and brown to highlight the natural origin of the ingredients.

Conclusions

Choosing the right colors in marketing is an essential component for creating an effective and memorable visual experience for consumers. Using color psychology, understanding the target audience, and maintaining visual consistency can significantly improve the impact of advertising campaigns.

9.Glossary of Color Marketing

Color marketing is a fundamental discipline in the world of branding and visual communication. Understanding the meaning and use of colors can make a difference in how a brand is perceived by consumers and in their emotional response to advertising campaigns. This glossary of color marketing explores key concepts, strategies, and psychological implications of colors in the context of marketing.

1. **Emotional Associations of Colors**

Colors evoke specific emotions and sensations that can profoundly influence consumer perception and behavior.

- **Red**: Symbolizes passion, energy, urgency. It is often used to grab attention and stimulate action.

- **Blue**: Represents trust, seriousness, calmness. Widely used in sectors requiring reliability and professionalism.

- **Green**: Evokes nature, health, sustainability. Associated with eco-friendly products and healthy lifestyles.

- **Yellow**: Symbolizes joy, optimism, creativity. It is attention-grabbing and communicates a sense of positivity.

- **Black**: Represents elegance, luxury, exclusivity. Often used for high-end products.

- **White**: Symbolizes purity, simplicity, cleanliness. It conveys clarity and order.

2. **Cultural Implications**

Associations with colors can vary significantly across cultures and regions. Considering the cultural implications of colors in global marketing strategies is essential to avoid misunderstandings.

- **Example**: Red is associated with luck and prosperity in many Asian cultures, while in the West, it may be interpreted as a color of passion or urgency.

3. **Psychology of Colors in Marketing**

Color psychology studies how colors influence consumer emotions, perceptions, and purchasing decisions.

- **Emotional Engagement**: Colors can evoke intense emotional reactions that influence consumer behavior.

- **Brand Perception**: Color choices can shape brand perception, conveying values, personality, and identity.

- **Competitive Differentiation**: Colors can help a brand stand out from the competition, creating a unique and recognizable visual identity.

4. **Color Choice in Branding**

In branding, colors are carefully selected to reflect the essence of the brand and positively influence consumer perceptions.

- **Visual Consistency**: Maintaining visual consistency across all branding materials to strengthen brand identity.

- **Reflection of Brand Values**: Chosen colors should align with the brand's values and mission.

- **Cultural Adaptability**: Considering how colors will be perceived in different cultures and adapting the global branding strategy accordingly.

5. **Use of Colors in Marketing Materials**

In marketing materials, colors are used to attract attention, communicate key messages, and stimulate consumer action.

- **Websites**: Color choices for websites impact user experience and brand perception online.

- **Logos**: Colors in logos are essential for creating a memorable and distinctive visual identity.

- **Packaging**: Packaging colors influence purchase decisions and communicate product features.

- **Promotional Materials**: Colors in flyers, brochures, and advertisements are used to capture attention and convey crucial information.

6. **Strategies for Color Selection**

Key strategies in color selection for marketing include:

- **Understanding the Target Audience**: Analyzing preferences and emotional reactions of the target audience to different colors.

- **A/B Testing**: Conducting tests to evaluate the effectiveness of different color combinations in advertising campaigns.

- **Metrics Monitoring**: Gathering feedback and analyzing performance metrics to continuously optimize the use of colors.

7. **Common Mistakes to Avoid**

- **Ignoring Cultural Implications**: Failing to consider how colors are perceived in different cultures can lead to misunderstandings of the brand message.

- **Lack of Visual Consistency**: Inconsistent use of colors can weaken the brand's visual identity.

- **Choosing Colors Based Solely on Personal Preferences**: Relying on personal preferences rather than considering branding and target audience considerations can compromise marketing effectiveness.

- **Not Testing Color Choices**: Neglecting to test and evaluate the effectiveness of color choices can result in missed opportunities for improvement and campaign optimization.

The glossary of color marketing provides an in-depth overview of key concepts, strategies, and implications of colors in marketing. Using colors strategically can significantly enhance the visual, emotional, and communicative impact of advertising campaigns, contributing to brand success and recognition. Understanding color psychology, considering cultural implications, and adapting color choices to the characteristics of the target audience are essential for creating an effective and memorable marketing strategy.

Effective Color Marketing Strategies: Enhancing Brand Impact

Color marketing plays a crucial role in shaping brand perception, influencing consumer behavior, and fostering emotional connections with the audience. To leverage colors effectively in marketing campaigns, it's essential to consider various strategies that align with brand identity, resonate with target audiences, and navigate cultural nuances. Here's an extensive guide outlining effective solutions for mastering color marketing:

Understanding the Psychology of Colors

1. **Emotional Associations**: Colors evoke specific emotions and perceptions. Understanding these associations—such as red for excitement and blue for trust—helps in choosing colors that resonate with the desired consumer sentiment.

2. **Cultural Sensitivity**: Colors hold diverse cultural meanings. For instance, while white symbolizes purity in Western cultures, it signifies mourning in some Asian cultures. Adapting colors to local cultural norms prevents unintended miscommunications.

3. **Color Harmonies**: Utilizing color harmonies (e.g., complementary, analogous) enhances visual appeal and readability. Harmonious color combinations create a cohesive and aesthetically pleasing brand image.

Strategies for Effective Color Selection

1. **Define Brand Identity**: Start by defining the brand's personality and values. Select colors that authentically reflect these traits. For instance, vibrant colors might suit a youthful and energetic brand, while muted tones convey sophistication.

2. **Target Audience Analysis**: Conduct thorough research on the target demographic's preferences and psychological responses to colors. This data-driven approach ensures that color choices resonate effectively with the intended audience.

3. **Competitive Analysis**: Analyze competitors' color strategies to identify gaps and opportunities for differentiation. Choosing unique colors or using existing colors in innovative ways can help the brand stand out in a crowded market.

4. **A/B Testing**: Test different color combinations and variations in controlled settings to measure consumer responses accurately. A/B testing provides empirical data to optimize color choices for maximum impact.

Implementing Colors Across Marketing Channels

1. **Branding and Logo Design**: Select colors for logos and branding materials that encapsulate the brand's essence. Consistency in color use across different touchpoints reinforces brand recognition and enhances brand recall.

2. **Website and Digital Presence**: Color choices on websites impact user experience and perception. Use colors strategically to guide users' attention, enhance readability, and evoke desired emotional responses.

3. **Packaging and Product Design**: Packaging colors influence purchasing decisions. Align packaging colors with product attributes (e.g., green for eco-friendly products) to communicate brand values and appeal to environmentally conscious consumers.

4. **Advertising and Promotional Materials**: Colors in advertisements should align with campaign objectives and resonate

with the target audience. Use colors to evoke emotions that drive consumer engagement and action.

Best Practices for Effective Color Marketing

1. **Consistency**: Maintain consistency in color usage across all marketing channels to strengthen brand identity and foster brand loyalty.

2. **Flexibility**: While consistency is key, allow for flexibility to adapt colors to specific cultural contexts or seasonal campaigns without compromising brand integrity.

3. **Accessibility**: Ensure color choices consider accessibility standards, making content inclusive and accessible to all users, including those with visual impairments.

4. **Monitor and Adapt**: Continuously monitor consumer feedback and performance metrics related to color usage. Adapt strategies based on insights to optimize marketing effectiveness over time.

Avoiding Common Pitfalls

1. **Ignoring Cultural Nuances**: Neglecting to consider cultural interpretations of colors can lead to unintentional misunderstandings or alienation of potential customers.

2. **Over-reliance on Trends**: While trendy colors can attract attention, they may not always align with the brand's long-term identity or resonate with the target audience.

3. **Personal Bias**: Avoid choosing colors based solely on personal preferences. Instead, prioritize colors that align with brand strategy and consumer preferences.

4. **Failure to Test**: Skipping A/B testing or not evaluating the impact of color choices can result in missed opportunities for optimization and improvement.

Conclusion

Effective color marketing is a nuanced art that combines psychological understanding, cultural sensitivity, strategic planning, and continuous optimization. By strategically leveraging colors across branding, digital channels, and promotional materials, brands can create compelling visual narratives that resonate with consumers, strengthen brand identity, and drive business success. Understanding the impact of colors and implementing thoughtful strategies ensures that every hue contributes meaningfully to the brand's story and consumer engagement.

Index

1.Introduction pg.4

2.Cultural Associations with Colors and Color Psychology pg.17

3.Psychological Effects of Colors on User Behavior pg.29

4.Practical Applications of Colors in Marketing pg.44

5.Use of Colors in Branding pg.58

6.Choosing Colors for Marketing Materials (Websites, Logos, Packaging, etc.) pg.73

7.Consequences of Color Choice in Advertising Campaigns pg.83

8.How to Choose the Right Colors and Avoid Mistakes pg.90

9.Glossary of Color Marketing pg.98